IT'S OKAY TO BE A GOOD GIRL

AUTHOR JAY DOUBLEU

Za-Van Gail Publishing

IT'S OK TO BE A
GOOD
GIRL

AUTHOR
JAY DOUBLEU

CONTENTS

To the millennium generation and beyond

INTRODUCTION

What is this book about?

It's about order, sophistication, permission, support, taking the covers off, choosing, embracing, and deciding. Also know this book is equally about the battle of morality VS freedom, right VS subjection, and wrong VS opinion. This fight often gets ugly while creating counterfeits of a reality created from going along to get along.

A girl/woman tries her best to listen to her God-given conscience in a world full of pressures to object "IT," the morality "IT" screams for, the good character "IT" produces, and the rules "IT" guides her to follow.

Rebellion influences the rejection of, and the protection of, imparted and taught standards that began at home in some cases. Those same rebellious influences also stand inopposition of the things her heart and her God-given conscience are bearing witness against in ALL cases.

What is the purpose of this book?

The purpose is to give YOU, yes YOU, permission to live a Godly life unapologetically. It is for YOU to feel unmoved by the pressure to submit to bad choices, for YOU to be reassured of your wholeness while living an exciting life that is honorable, and for YOU to have a clear understanding of how important respect is at YOUR core. Know that YOU are empowered to have standards!

YOU will become comfortable with using the word "no." YOU will discover the strength to go against the tide, and ultimately be okay with the title of "Good Girl," resting in the fact that YOU are anything but boring.

Know morality will secure YOUR reputation from rumors, and will have YOUR back when someone attempts to question YOUR character, even if YOU are not in the room. Morality provides a more complete protection to YOU by training YOUR ear to harken to its pleading of a yield, stop, go, or no. Morality and ethics are not a prison. They are defenses from the enemy's often clever offense of just the opposite. These safeguards will prove to be your rest.

IT

Designed to guide you Protect you, support you Point you in
the right direction
But you're in opposition of it. Our society is attempting to
override it
Quiet it Reprogram it Totally rebuild it.
But they can't, because... See, they didn't design it.
It can be corrupted if you simply bend to it.
Don't listen to it.
Ignore it
Or count it as a nuisance.
It's called your conscious.
It's defined as being aware of what one is doing.
So you can't trick it, manipulate it, or fake it Or tell it that
you're mistaken.
It's your conscious and God created it.
She knew that wasn't her husband.

He knew that wasn't his wife.

You wanted the money, that's why you took that life.

That was her idea but you took it to get paid.

Now you say her poverty is her own sad maze You won't get off that easy; no one else will be to blame.

So you can call it a snitch, if you will It won't cover for you.

You can even call it a tattle tale.

And it's still going to tell the truth.

You won't be able to deny it spoke to you.

It's your conscious and it will either speak against or for you.

On that Day of Judgment, which one will yours do?

We squeal like girls do upon seeing one another.

"Oh my goodness, it's so good to see you, Shayla!" We walk over to a nearby bench and have a seat. Shayla and I are both here at this bowling alley, trying to get rid of "the lonlies." This is just part of the process of divorce we are both enduring. I am so thankful for this meet up! It gives me a chance to do just that while allowing me to get out of the house, and more importantly, out of my head.

"I know, it's good to see you, too, Jay! You been okay?" "Yes. I've been getting things together." Shayla says, "Me too. Lately, I have been trying to relax, let go, and enjoy my life. I've always been known as the 'good girl.' You know?"

She crosses her legs and leans back. I take her cue to relax and lean back, too. But I immediately pop back up at attention and respond after her statement has an opportunity to sink in.

"I totally understand that!" I let out a sigh of irritation. My whole body reacts! Who knows what my face is doing?!

We both laugh and Shayla continues. "I've had this friend since high school and she's always getting high. I've decided I'm giving myself permission to live a little. So ... I finally called her up and told her I wanted to try it. "

"What? Shayla! No!" I think to myself, we're too old for that! At the same time, I secretly think of how I would never have the nerve to do it. Even at this age, I can still hear my mom's warning as well as all of the D.A.R.E programs I'd sat through! Stay away from drugs!

She then sits up straight and leans toward me to make sure she isn't talking too loud. After all, there are still other people sitting near us. "I'm serious, Jay. I'm just going to enjoy my life and let go."

I lean in a little more as well to ensure our continued confidentiality. I tell her about my newfound openness. I tell her how "my good girl lifestyle" is no longer something she has to worry about.

She says, "Well, girl just in case the 'good girl' shows back up, we aren't going to waste any of the good weed on your behind. I'll just have to find someone that sells the cheap stuff!"

Shayla and I both burst out laughing! She says she'll let me know when she gets the weed. It doesn't take her long. She calls me back within a week of our conversation.

Jay she tells me, "I can't find any cheap weed. You will just have to smoke the good stuff!"

I think I'm worth it. We continue to laugh. She invites me over, along with some of our other friends on a Saturday evening. I arrive and it's obvious the party has already started. Thick smoke fills the room. Everyone is laughing so hard and seems to really be enjoying themselves.

When I see everyone letting loose, I know I've made the right decision. It's time for me to be laughing, as well. No more "good girl." As I walk over to the table to become a part of the scene, relief is the only thing on my mind. I reach for the fattest joint in front of me. I take a hit of the weed, and guess what?!

Nothing happens! Absolutely nothing happens. We start to lose it, laughing almost uncontrollably. My friend urges me to take another hit. So, I actually take a few more puffs. I then realize that it is still having NO EFFECT ON ME! I mean none! By this time, we are not containing ourselves. People around us are staring, probably wondering what the heck is so funny!

I say to her, "Now that's funny!" Shayla replies, "I had to try it one last time just to make sure, and guess what? Nothing still!"

My next statement changes the tone of our dialogue to a serious one as I reply, "No, that was God protecting you from yourself."

I could tell this woke her up a bit. She isn't laughing anymore as she answers, "You're probably right."

We continued to laugh and talk about other things, but our exchange stuck with me because I, too, was struggling with being that "good girl." And let me just say, I wasn't doing so hot with that whole "good girl" thing either. At that time, my divorce had been finalized just over a year.

I was attempting to live for God and do the right thing while my hormones were craving a guy I'd been dating. And let me just put the truth out there: he had definitely been satisfying my cravings. I should have been able to resist. I knew that the relationship was wrong. I had no business even being in another relationship, let alone that type of relationship.

Every time we had sex, my conscience grew heavier and heavier. I had no peace with my behavior. But I have to be honest, it was what I wanted. My desire often overrode what I knew was right to do.

Shayla was a divorcee, as well. As you can see, she was also battling with doing her best to have fun while laboring to keep her values and morals intact, not to mention attempting to find her way through this very warped 21st century dating scene. We got that about each other.

My body was still present with Shayla. However, in that moment, I somewhat zoned out. Not only did the magnitude of her statement about being tired of being a good girl stick with me, it also dove even deeper into my heart and beckoned to me to listen to what it had to say.

My heart began to ask me questions. What was going

too far for someone like me? How could I have fun, be trendy, and not lose my mind?

My mind replied, I honestly haven't thought that out yet. Shayla and I continued to sit there in that crowded bowling alley as we continued to share our lives with one another. Our experiences gave me insight into the face that we were struggling with who we were, or at least supposed to be. It then became even clearer; we were simply two "good girls" trying to figure it out.

"What were we trying to figure out?" you may ask.

Where should the "good girl" boundaries lie? What is okay for us to do? Does our morality make us boring?

I just knew that if someone did not answer those questions for us, we would surely lose ourselves in what the world wanted us to do. Every "good girl" would, because these "good girls" already were. And the world would make sure we knew that "right" did not have to be our only choice, because OUR CHOICES could be made right. Right?

NOTES

Date:_____Time:_____Mood:_____

_____
_____
_____
_____
_____
_____
_____
_____
_____
_____
_____
_____
_____
_____
_____
_____

Chapter One

WHAT IS A GOOD GIRL? VALUES, MORALS & UPBRINGING

*R*ead this until you get it: THIS BOOK IS NOT A JUDGMENT CALL, IT IS A CALL TO JUDGMENT REGARDING WHO YOU ARE, WHAT YOU ARE DOING, AND WHY YOU ARE DOING IT AS A GIRL, OR AS A WOMAN!

What is a "good girl?" A good girl is defined as a girl that has values and morals that tend to guide her actions, decisions, and attitudes. In most cases, she has been raised to wait until she gets married to have sex, and tries to live by that as much as possible. This girl may have been raised in a church, or at minimum with adherence to a strict moral code which taught her that God honors her obedience and watches over her carefully.

In addition, she believes in treating people right in the face of being treated wrong. She also gets good grades in school because she knows that she doesn't have a reason not

1

to, as well as knowing that her parents demand it. Her parents won't accept less. And as an additional side note, her parents better not get a call from her teachers, or else!

If you have been raised as a "good girl," your mother has taught you that it is not appropriate for you to expose too much of your breasts or behind. This straightforward principal has been ingrained, and was supported by your biblical teaching.

Also due to that teaching, your God-given conscience is not only alive in you, but you know when it is speaking to you. Don't lie. Be honest. Don't you dare sneak around to wear that make-up! He is not the one! Have you lost your whole mind?!

In our society, right and wrong are a gigantic mixed bag of subjectivity. The perception of wrong and right mainly gets based upon by the one making the rules, which is usually ... YOU! And we know when YOU make the rules, anything YOU do or say can be justified or rationalized to be done or not done because of YOUR feelings, the advanJ tage the situation will give YOU, or for the satisfaction of YOU being "right."

You feel the weight of living in a world to object your morals, standards, and good character; you are encouraged to break the rules, along with the influence to rebel against the restriction and the protection of those imparted and taught standards that were instilled at home in some cases, whereas in other cases, you already instinctively knew better.

YOU ACT LIKE ONE

One Thursday night, a friend of mine and I decided to step out. There was a lounge-type bar known to be jumping, even on a weeknight, so we decided to try it out. Neither one of us had been there before, but we wanted a break from the day-to-day routine. After all, we were both fairly single, and our love lives were stale.

My friend, Cree, agreed to drive us there because I don't drive on the freeway. On the way, she expressed she was not going to set any expectations on the evening. As we pulled up, I agreed, knowing what I wanted would not be there anyway. I was missing my old life. It hit me at the oddest times.

Cree parked the car and we got out. Walking up to the door of the place only emphasized my feelings of loss. I pushed those feelings down so I could enjoy the evening.

We stepped into the lounge and it was full! I don't know

why I was surprised, because the fact it took us nearly ten minutes to park should have been the tell-all. The bar was our first destination once we got inside, and it became the perfect place for me to plant. It offered a great view of the room so one could people-watch without getting accused of rudely staring.

As the night went on, my friend and I met some gentlemen and began to talk and laugh with them, Cree more than me. I wasn't as tuned in as I could have been. My head just was not there.

About an hour and a half passed. The crowd started to die down within the bar, and people began to move out to the parking lot to continue their conversations. Here in Texas, the parking lot is known as your last chance to mack, get a phone number, and see what people really look like without the flattering club light.

I started to notice how late it was getting. Had Cree forgotten it was a work night?! She had downed four Crown and Cokes by that time, so I knew the late hour was not on her mind. I tried to give some subtle verbal clues that it was time to go, but it was clear she wanted to continue talking to the gentlemen we had met inside.

His friend and I somehow struck up a conversation. And trust me; it was not, nor was it going to be, a "hook up" opportunity at all. Especially not with the condition he was in. He was tipsy. Not drunk, just on his way there.

In his buzzed state, he began to talk about the girl he

had been dealing with. She had done a number on him, and the hurt was evident.

Women take note! I have to say this, if you don't already know: when a man gets hurt, he fights back verbally, among other things. They can be just as vicious as women can be with their mouths.

So of course, at that time, he could find nothing good to say about her. She was everything but what her mother named her. I could not believe I let him say some of the things which poured from his mouth. I knew that if I were to correct him, he would've found me out, because normally the Minister part of me would have shown up and I would have rebuked his behind. But that night, I just smiled kindly and picked up that he needed to get it out.

He looked over my shoulder to see if his friend was done talking with mine. He and I began to walk over to where they were to interrupt them. We could see that our presence was not wanted by the way they stared at us and silence fell, so I walked over to our car to sit down. He followed.

"Hey, did you hear what I said earlier?" he asked, seemingly a little more sober.

Yes, I thought, I did hear you whining and throwing a tantrum. But I didn't say that. Trust, whoever that girl was, she had put him through enough!

For sake of the story, I will call him "Ted," since clearly me going to the car did not tell him our conversation was over. Ted then began to share once more.

Okay, here we go, I thought. Round Two!

But this time, Ted began to talk about how much he really liked the same girl he'd just called out her name for nearly an hour, which was a total tune change! At some point, Ted even apologized for his language from our prior exchange. He kept going. After about thirty to forty-five more minutes, he stopped talking suddenly and looked at me.

He said, "I bet you're a minister." I could have just spit! I wish I could've seen the look on my face. Several thoughts ran across my mind. Seriously. A minister? All of that lusciousness I was showing and he still found me out? The boobs were out, for goodness sakes! Was he for real?! I was so outdone. I laughed and nodded my head in agreement. I just surrendered in that moment.

He said, "I knew it! See what I mean? There is no hiding who you really are. You act like one."

The reality of his words hit me hard. However, I began to understand his statement. The revelation immediately came, even in the pursuit to seem like everybody else around me, I couldn't hide. Even in the attire I was wearing or the lounge I was in. Somehow my disposition did not match, and it was my disposition that gave me away.

One definition of disposition is: the way in which something is placed or arranged, especially in relation to other things.

In other words, with all that was going on, the way I held myself and my response was placed and arranged in such a way that in relation to others around me, I displayed something different. In my mind, I was propped up just like at least fifty percent of the females there. My makeup was just as cute. My hairstyle was equally as current as everyone else's, too. Therefore, no one should have been able to detect the difference.

Let emphasize that "good girl", you are different. But I do not want you to take that difference as a punishment (although I did in that moment until I really began to understand.) The good girl aroma is like a state-of-the-art alarm system to a million-dollar mansion. It keeps the crazies out if you let it. You need to know that you won't be popular like "that" ... "that" meaning mainstream popularity. But it will cause you to be respected like "that" ... "that" meaning respect for who you are and what you are.

This is the trade-off many times; be respected, or be known for twenty-four hour access. In other words, be a woman with ethics or not. You choose. As you read the remainder of this book, you will choose.

You will have to choose if you want to have the type of fun where you will be able to look yourself in the mirror, or be the fun that has you questioning your identity. Your choice.

Once again, I will reiterate that you will have to choose if you want to be known for standards, or popularity. Your choice.

You will have to choose if you want to struggle with the consequences premarital sex can yield, or have the peace waiting until marriage will bring. Your choice.

Are you willing to be what some people consider the odd-ball? Your choice.

If you have already chosen unwisely, are you willing to make an about-face? You still have a choice.

If you have already given away your virtue more times than you care to admit, the question is, "Do you want to stop?" You still have a choice.

If you have wasted time in your life, God can redeem it. Ask Him to do it. You still have a voice and more importantly, a choice.

Read this until you get it: THIS BOOK IS NOT A JUDGMENT CALL, IT IS A CALL TO JUDGMENT REGARDING WHO YOU ARE, WHAT YOU ARE DOING, AND WHY YOU ARE DOING IT ... AS A GIRL, OR AS A WOMAN!

Whatever you choose, choose wisely. Some choices have consequences which can be costly.

NOTES

Date:_____Time:_____Mood:_____

_____
_____
_____
_____
_____
_____
_____
_____
_____
_____
_____
_____
_____
_____
_____
_____

Chapter Two

THE STRUGGLE THAT A GOOD GIRL HAS: GOD VS. GOOD SEX

I kiss him and a surge of burning heat literally runs throughout my body in record time. I'd never even felt this from my husband when I kissed him. Is this just lust, or is this my second chance at love? I couldn't be ready to love yet, could I?

Let me be clear. Up until this point, I have not been touched in nearly three to four months. My current reality is that my husband has chosen his mistress over his commitment. The divorce wasn't even final and yet he's fully engaged in another relationship. So, if he can play, why can't I?

At this time, I've missed everything that a man has to offer; the way they smell, the deepness in a man's voice that has the ability to make me moist, and the touch of a man's God-given strength that no woman can ever match. That strength was security to me.

So this kiss is perhaps just a kiss to him, but to me it says that somebody wants me. This "Want" equals "Love," even if it is not the person that I want the love from. It's better than nothing. He wants me, so ... he ... loves ... me. Right?

"You are so beautiful." He kisses me again on my lips while moving his hands to my thighs. It caused an eruption within me. His arms embrace my waist as his hands then move on to hold the center of my back. In every word that proceeds out of his mouth, he seems to encourage my exisJ tence as a woman.

Once again, Nathan calls me beautiful. Is this just another pickup line? The thought does cross my mind. If so, he's just picked me up.

Like I said, it has been a nearly six months since my husband decided he wanted another woman. The pain is still fresh. It's like my pain has been put into a Ziploc bag. Troy, my husband, simply told me that he was leaving me, went out of town to continue working, and did not come back.

But before I knew he wasn't coming back, I'd hoped that maybe he would come back home and choose me. It is now Memorial Day weekend of 2012, and for sure, the certainty that he is not returning has been secured by the fact that I'd learned he'd spent the weekend with his mistress and her family. He was not coming back, and I was not his choice.

PAIN & ANGER HAVE A BEHAVIOR

The pain from that news was real, but it also "justified" my actions. I had no problem mounting Nathan later, because my anger at God and my then-husband was an understatement which fueled my actions. And I was not going to be through any time soon. If this was the result, I would create my own reward.

The need for someone to hold me was real. Yeah, I get it and this "good girl" knows; legally, I was still married. But no one else seemed to notice. Did I still have to do the right thing, or be a "good girl?" Because he sure wasn't being a "good boy" (but I guess that's another story).

I was a "good girl" and good wife. This was not supposed to happen to me. Ten years I stood by him while he couldn't get a steady job! I protected his secrets! I had broken the should-have-been fall of this man's reputation one too many times! Was this really my reward for all my faithfulness and loyalty? You have got to be kidding!

Nathan and I continued being a thing, and I continued getting my affirmation from him. He held me close whenever I needed it. Deep down, I knew it had to stop. But, his touch was gentle and reassuring. Each kiss he gave me made me desire for another, yet it scared me. In as much as I did not want to acknowledge it, this relationship was like a drug. My body was NOT supposed to yearn for him. Every thought of him caused a reaction inside of my stomach and between my legs.

Wrong or right, I kept seeing him, and the moistness kept happening when he came near me. Did I sleep with Nathan over and over and over and over and over? Yes, I did. Was it right? No, it wasn't. My conscience, morals, standards and ethics were trying to counsel me, but I was tired of being counseled and I was tired of being the "good girl." Been tired.

Due to the fact I was not listening to the trio at this time *(my morality, ethics, or standards)*, I had come to the conclusion that I wasn't a "good girl" anymore. This decision was apart of the fight. Was it going to be this man or my God? My God VS Nathan's Good Sex? This one thought would return to me many times. Did the decision really need to be made between those two? The fact I felt like I had to ask tore me apart. Nevertheless, God knew that I loved Him, but I also craved Nathan. In this moment had to face a hard truth; my cravings had become equal with God in my life.

Let's be real here: I knew the sex was not going to heal me, but at the time, it was the reminder of my beauty and the actuality of still very much being someone's choice that fed me. In hindsight, I know now that relationship was just as much about me being Nathan's choice as it was about the physical intimacy. I had to learn this lesson about myself so I could deal with the effects of rejection and anger due to a failed marriage.

This experience was not supposed to end up in this book, but I can't neglect to tell you vividly how intense my struggle was mentally, physically, and spiritually regarding being the "good girl" that I was when I was a once-married woman, as well as giving you an authentic look inside to how my anger and pain were acting out. There is no way I am going to let you think that this "good girl" did not become the puppet of her trauma.

Some will probably wonder if am I am somehow glorifying what I did. The answer is noooo, I'm not. I am being open and honest. In order to teach it, I must tell it like it is. Remember what you read back at the beginning of chapter one: THIS BOOK IS NOT A JUDGMENT CALL, IT IS A BOOK TO CALL TO JUDGMENT WHO YOU ARE, WHAT YOU ARE DOING, AND WHY YOU ARE DOING IT ... AS A GIRL, OR AS A WOMAN!

I am human. I say that not as an excuse to do wrong, but so you can understand that my carnality was the place I was living from, not my spirit or my faith. This fact is never an easy self-truth to accept. Yet, it is a truth many of us must be willing to receive about ourselves. If not, then living from a place of carnality without the understanding of that is indeed what is happening will continually excuse you and justify you every time. And that will serve no one well.

After a year into the relationship, my moral compass became the reason I could no longer endure screwing Nathan in peace. The pain and anger of my ex husband's rejection had caused me to nurse its effects in a medication that wasn't prescribed for it. Many of us know this prescription all too well. For many, being injured to that magnitude causes blurred lines in everyday decision making where normally there would be none. Unfortunately, when this happens, the outcome is loss of precious time, a peace of mind, and self. I lost me. I lost time. I did not have a peace of mind. Not to mention I discovered addiction. I had not known addiction before this.

I did not desire to deal with the pain, just like you, so the pain did what I was giving it permission to do by not dealing with it properly, while taking my sex- medication. This is why I have come into a full comprehension of why lawyers can legally build defenses off of the actions of behavior triggered by trauma. Often times, pain and anger truly do act out *without* the clarity of sound thinking!

Many "good girls" who have been faithful wives or girl-friends, good mothers, and loyal spouses get sucked into emotional despair after the trauma of being betrayed and left and rejected. It takes all their moral minds to not go out and become the biggest whores of the states they live in.

They face becoming the h** they've gossiped about a time or two, or even becoming the identical homewrecker that wrecked their homes.

Agony changes us. You become unrecognizable to yourself. Your standards will shift from its normal baseline.

But many "good girls" would say or mistakenly think, "I won't go too far," or, "That is not me."

I understand how those statements are easy to declare when your morality isn't being challenged by anger and pain. I was a "good girl," I wouldn't do that ... or could I? Mmm, but wasn't I already doing it? Sounds confusing; it can be, but the truth is agony employs us.

I have tested the old adage of "getting under a new one will help you get over the old one," but I discovered that advice was all about the physical part of a person. Physical actions only take your intellect to do, not your heart. So, while your heart is continuing to break from the damage you've experienced, you're physically just simply performing.

Know this: anyone can physically perform. All the while your spirit is weeping. The functionality of one-third of anything can be acceptable. However, two- thirds of something is over half, and that's too much of you functioning out of anguish to be acceptable.

THERE IS NOTHING NEW

David, a man we famously know for being a man after God's own heart...

Acts 13:22 tells us that God removed Saul and replaced him with David, a man about whom God said, "I have found David, son of Jesse, a man after my own heart. He will do everything I want him to do."

That just moves me! God had confidence in David's obedience, although He knew the weakness of his flesh and character.

But David! Oh, King David! 2 Samuel 11:2-4 explains how when King David saw Bathsheba bathing on top of the roof, he saw how incredibly beautiful she was and he sent his men to go get her, even after finding out she was indeed married! See scripture below:

*² One evening, David got up from his bed and walked
around on the roof of the palace. From the roof,
he saw a woman bathing. The woman was very
beautiful,*

*³ and David sent someone to find out about her. The
man said, "She is Bathsheba, the daughter of
Eliam and the wife of Uriah the Hittite."*

*⁴ Then David sent messengers to get her. (Now she
was purifying herself from her monthly
uncleanness.) Then she went back home.*

When what we like and desire is before us while also being **accessible** to us, we tend to go after it, **whether right or wrong.** David did it then. We do it now. David pursued Bathsheba initially without the moral struggle, just as we do. The truth is this: most often, pleasure wins out over morality.

Let me bring me it home a little more... Eating gives the consumer a lot of warm fuzzies. Those fuzzies come from the look, the smell, the experience, and or the anticipation of the taste alone. But how frequently do you think of what the result might be from what you are going to eat, or the result it will have on your body first? This is because the real conviction of what you ate, or the behavior itself, does not set in until you've really had a chance to think about it. First things first, you are just ready to partake in the moment. We want the experience.

As David's story progresses, the scripture tells us how

David laid with Bathsheba. They were intimate. Then David discovers as a consequence of being with Bathsheba, she has become pregnant! After all, the baby was not her husband's! The servants knew it, and David knew it. Right after that, David arranges to have her husband, Uriah, killed! Not just any kind of way, but in battle. David was attempting to have her husband killed doing his job so it could not be questioned, and with this he would not have to face Uriah for what he had done. Sure enough, David sent him into battle, and Uriah died in battle. After his death, David brings Bathsheba to his home and she becomes one of his wives, according to 2 Samuel 11:22-26.

> [22] *So the messenger went to Jerusalem and gave a complete report to David.*
> [23] *"The enemy came out against us in the open fields," he said. "And as we chased them back to the city gate,*
> [24] *the archers on the wall shot arrows at us. Some of the king's men were killed, including Uriah the Hittite."*
> [25] *"Well, tell Joab not to be discouraged," David said. "The sword devours this one today and that one tomorrow! Fight harder next time, and conquer the city!"*
> [26] *When Uriah's wife heard that her husband was dead, she mourned for him.*
> [27] *When the period of mourning was over, David sent*

for her and brought her to the palace, and she became one of his wives.

Pay close attention, because there are no verses conveying repentance from David at first. A man after God's own heart, you would think we would have read about some type of remorse a little sooner than what we do. But verse twenty-seven reads, "When the period of mourning was over, David sent for her and brought her to the palace, and she became one of his wives."

Once again, we read about the mourning of a wife for her husband, not the regret of a king, and certainly not a man who loves God madly! Not long after, she gave birth to a son. But the word of God expresses how displeased the Lord was with what David had done.

In 2 Samuel chapter 12, you will see where God sent a prophet to tell David a story which angers David. The prophet Nathan tells David about a rich man who had a guest arrive at his home, and instead of killing an animal from his own herd, he killed an animal from a poor man's flock. David became furious, the Bible says! David then says, "As surely as the Lord lives, he vowed any man who would do such a thing deserves to die! He must repay four lambs to the poor man for the one he stole and for having no pity!

Then the prophet Nathan says, "David, you are that man!"

"Boom!" as my husband says. The prophet goes on, and around verses thirteen through twenty of 2 Samuel 12, we see the remorse conveyed by David and the consequences for King David's actions he begins to reap.

What's my point? My point is our fleshly desires and/or our insatiable appetite to want has always waged war against our better judgment and convictions. God VS Good Sex, versus Beauty, versus Money, versus Power, and versus Position (to name a few) have always gotten us tripped up, resulting in a loss of integrity, beauty, money, power, position, and more, which are all the SAME things we sacrificed everything for to begin with.

This is the crux of the issue. Desires (in my case Good Sex) VS morality (GOD) won't be able to be chosen correctly until we decide beforehand, which means before the temptation arrives. I mean, you and I have to really decide that compromising is not an option, especially when it removes you from the will of God.

Subsequently, after you make that decision, you are going to also need to ensure that YOU make it a point to learn YOU. Ask God to show you YOU. This is the only way you are going to know what you are earnestly made of, or capable of. One can't know their heart in its entirety. However, they can become familiar with it, how it makes decisions, how it deals with feelings, and most of all how it deals with the pressures of life.

You can also gain a perspective filled with wisdom concerning your heart which will allow you to know when God is giving you time to flee a situation that could cause you to sin, put you in harm's way, or a temptation which will overcome your weakness, creating life-altering distractions.

In Jeremiah 17:9, it reads that the heart is deceitful above all things. Who can know it? You and I won't know our hearts completely because our hearts will forever surprise us.

David saw how beautiful Bathsheba was. But, he wanted her. David knew immediately upon the return of his men he'd sent to inquire of her that she was married. But, he wanted her. An innocent man died. But, he wanted her.

Hey, good girl, what do you want? No, I mean for real. What would you see "bathing" that would make you, a girl who is known for being one with morals and standards, kill and plot to get it, consequently jeopardizing your reputation and your position with God?

What secret desire are you battling with? Do you have a problem with being told no? Do you have a problem with boundaries? Do you fight against being wanted? Is money your vice?

You gotta know YOU, good girl. You better decide, good girl. You must know your vice!

NOTES

Date:_____Time:_____Mood:_____

_____

_____

_____

_____

_____

_____

_____

_____

_____

_____

_____

_____

_____

_____

_____

_____

_____

_____

Chapter Three

PRESSURE BURSTS A PIPE

Poetic Truth
While you sit under the weight of expectation and the
words of "wake up and pay attention,"
no one seems to mention that there is something that you are supposed to
be doing.
So, as you crumple like balled up paper because so much is being
demanded,
your conscience is being caught red-handed, handing your morals an
eviction notice.
You know you are only going to be some people's type ...
remember that the pressure to appeal to everyone is the same pressure
that can surely burst a pipe!

&

*A*s you read this chapter, let these questions be ones you refuse to remain unanswered in your heart:

1. What pressure are you putting on yourself? 2. Who or where are other pressures coming from? 3. Why are you accepting them?

Matthew 11:28-30 (MSG) reads,

> *"Are you tired? Worn out? Burned out on religion?*
> *Come to me. Get away with me and you'll*
> *recover your life. I'll show you how to take a real*
> *rest. Walk with me and work with me—watch*
> *how I do it. Learn the unforced rhythms of grace.*
> *I won't lay anything heavy or ill-fitting on you.*
> *Keep company with me and you'll learn to live*
> *freely and lightly."*

"Okay, Zee, she did not tell me she did hair out of her home. Should we go in?"

My daughter Zee stares at me without saying a word. I know it's getting late. I don't like being between a rock and a hard place! I look over to my daughter while telling her, "Your pageant activities start in just a little while. We really don't have a choice. Dang it! I guess we got to deal with it."

We walk up to the door. My last thought before the door opens is, God, please don't let this blow up in my face. I should have done more research.

As she answers the door, I (without hesitation) express my surprise of the salon being "here," at her home.

She says, "I thought you knew." She then asks, "Did you see the ad?"

I think to myself, this is what I get for listening to Tracy's behind! Never again! I answer, "No ma'am, I did not. Do you have a license?"

"Yes." I look over to my right where my daughter is standing. I ask her, "Zee, you good?" I want to gauge her comfort level with the situation. "Yes, ma'am." "Well okay, I guess we are in this," I say to them both as we walk in to get started. However, I am saying to myself, let me see one wrong thing and we are going to be out of here so fast!

As the initial shock begins to wear off about this "home salon," we all start to chat a bit. Grace offers us something to drink and makes sure we feel comfortable. As I look around, I do have to say it is fairly clean. Nothing out of the ordinary or anything that would throw red flags.

Grace starts to open up the dialogue even more. She is very open, as most hairstylists are, and definitely a talker. I can't lie; it does allow for the situation to be less awkward as we sit in the home salon.

Grace wastes no time giving thanks to God and talking about her very personal journey back to Him. She's refreshingly open about what a tough fight it has been for her, but one that she is grateful for. Grace's heart needed to be heard, and since she was laying it all on the table that sat between us, I was there to listen. God needed me to hear what His spirit was saying.

For me personally, every twist and turn of a person's life holds my attention. What people manage to make it through just sits me still. Their resilience encourages me. I allow their lessons learned to teach me. Having said that, you must know the story that she would tell me about her daughter would not only sit me still, encourage me and teach me, but take my breath away.

"This is your daughter?" Grace asks. "Yes. My only one. She has just turned twenty." "Twenty?! She looks so young!" My daughter responds and tells her she gets that all the time.

"I have three kids; two boys and one girl," Grace says. "My daughter, Camry, has just graduated and moved to Dallas." Her voice conveys disappointment.

Her next statement would allow me to understand why. She says that Camry has dropped out of college after only one semester, and she's working in Dallas now with no family nearby. It worries and hurts her all at the same time. Grace wanted more for Camry.

Only a parent can understand the results to be reaped from making these types of life choices, because we as parents have at some level lived them. We would prefer for our children not to repeat our stupidity. Children have no idea how long it takes to get back motivated to pursuing an education once you've given it up. Some people never make it back, not to mention living in a place where there is no one around to have your back, and now all you have is one semester of college education and a minimum wage job. And as a parent, the following questions haunt us: who are you hanging around? What about your plan? I don't know any of your friends!

Grace continues. "I have been asking her to come back home and Camry keeps saying no. She always tells me, 'Mom, my life has been boring. Everyone I know has an interesting life story. I don't have one. I have always done the right thing. I want to have my own interesting life story to share.'"

Grace's voice begins to break. One could not ignore the hurt in this mom's voice, but Grace never broke her stride in doing Zee's hair. She was almost done straightening it.

My daughter chimes in, agreeing with Grace while letting her know her daughter was NOT the only one. She says many of her friends feel the same way and it is a very real and serious issue for some of them.

Zee continues, "Mama, many of them are depressed and feel worthless. They excitement-seek. I often hear them say they feel like they're missing something, that the frustraJ tion of being good is overwhelming! They don't feel like they can relate to others. A lot of them end up staring in the face of things they could have never imagined. They don't want to be good girls."

I began thinking, what in the heck?! That broke me. My daughter was attending a very well-known Christian univer-sity at this time.

At the point we were having this conversation, I had stopped writing this book. I knew that I should have already completed it. But it was clear that God was using her story to get my attention and encourage me to get going again. This is what He wanted me to hear.

The thought of any of our daughters forfeiting sound advice, safety, and guidance for "an interesting life story to tell" or "to have an experience" was too heavy to shoulder. Time was running out.

Correction, my time was running out. Write it. Tell them, so our daughters won't have to learn the hard way that it's all a lie. What's a lie? The pursuit to get the story they want ... it will cost them more than they are willing to pay. The title of this book came to mind like a much-needed slap in the face as Grace went on to reveal more of her life to us.

Grace went on to tell us how Camry was now getting the "life story" she wanted. She barely had any money. She owed for student loans since she had dropped out of school. She now had a boyfriend she was living with and **with that** Camry was now responsible for running a household and **with that** came having to act like a wife. You could tell from Grace's tone that her daughter was getting more than she'd bargained for. Camry was tired, yet she was determined to stick it out.

"Camry has made it clear to me that she is not coming home anytime soon."

Grace continues doing Zee's hair. Once again, she did

not let the telling of her story sidetrack her. I could tell Camry dropping out hurt Grace greatly, but not as much as the decisions she was enduring now. Grace had reached her limit of sharing. She began to omit other details of Camry's journey.

To hear more for me was not necessary. I wholeheartedly understood. I thought to myself, what was her story now lacking? Why wouldn't she just come home? But deep down, I knew why; home was safe, and she did not want safe right now. I wished Camry were there. I began to genuinely think about Camry's description to her mom before she left for college about her life being boring because she had always done the "right thing," and how Camry was over being a "good girl."

Then I got pissed! I wonder who told her that her life was boring, *which equally implied she was boring*. Whoever said it, she believed them. But why? What credibility did they have to make such a misled quality-call on her life? Maybe it was no one. Maybe it was everyone. Maybe it was her. One thing for sure: the person wasn't qualified.

There is something that tragically happens often in our society which I have coined as the "good girl assassination." The good girl assassination occurs when a girl/woman chooses to have values, or to have a sense of direction or even standards, but gets bullied with the pressure to shorten her skirt or face the threat of being considered a prude, or gets pushed to sleep with the star of the football team and maybe his friends so she will be popular, or perhaps the silent badge of honor she is told she will get to sleep with the celebrity in town for a night to have a "story to tell."

The assassination of a "good girl's" standards, values, and morals takes place through many subtle ways, like the way the writers of our most popular sitcoms write as they skillfully redefine a woman's definition of ethics, or as they try to make the displaying of promiscuity comfortable, not to mention the numerous advertisements which consistently convey how alternative lifestyles will free YOU from an "imprisoned state of living."

The strain to fit in, give in, or be a part of what is current is real!

And when a good girl does not comply, she risks the chance of being socially murdered if she chooses to say NO and uphold righteousness. John 10:10 says, "The thief's (the devil/enemy) PURPOSE is to STEAL, KILL, AND DESTROY."

One of the ways stealing, killing, and destroying occurs is when you start to see very key staples of morality stolen in our society (which is happening right before our eyes) from the original way it was intended, and then reassigned to an alternate way of thinking. An alternate way of thinking launches an alternate way of living. So, the devil actively persists to separate integrity from morality.

Please allow me to break this down a little more for easier consumption.

Morality is defined as right or virtuous conduct. Everyone knows that right or virtuous conduct is driven by our conscience, also known as the small voice within us, which tries to and responsible for directing us.

Universally, we ALL know good and bad this way, as an intuitive feeling. This even transcends cultural beliefs and training. The premise of right and wrong is weighed consciously within us first. The conscious God created in each of us is responsible for doing the inner work. Then the work of the conscious is supposed to be supported by sound teaching which registers with our intellect. Sound teaching then becomes a part of our intelligence.

Take the word "integrity" for example. It is defined as adherence to moral and ethical principles or soundness of moral character. In other words, obedience to a standard. What standard? The standard we instinctively know and the standard we have been taught in most instances. Although some may not even be biblically based, but morally based.

So, if we make morality about conduct (behavior), and leave out the standard of virtue, then morality can be negotiated. Likewise with integrity; remove ethics and then it becomes about the behavior. And again, if my behavior is not seemingly harmful, how can it be wrong? Then any objection of one's behavior alone would be considered hate without the weight of a moral or ethical component to measure it against.

Ultimately, morality would then be subjective to who is making the rules. This is all a part of the enemy's reprogramming of the conscience so that we get more and more comfortable with violating it. Once the violation happens, the behavior follows suit. And because the devil knows that God is not a man that He should lie, His word promises that He will give us over to a reprobate mind because of consistent disobedience to His word, which I will state once more is directly woven into our consciences when we ALL were created by God.

Destruction will be the outcome if our minds are turned over to live the way we see fit. Our lives will yield the destruction of our choices, lack of wisdom, and unwillingness to listen. Trace your steps backward in your own life and see if you don't see a trend of this. Bad choices, plus no wisdom, plus an unwillingness to listen, equal destruction.

(PAUSE AND THINK ABOUT IT.) You should know, just as I do, that when we do it our way, it ends the way an unGodly way would! My questions to you are: what areas do the pressures of life burst your pipes? What does your trend say?

BE AWARE

Instead of respecting value systems, a sense of direction, standards and morals for what they add, we count them as moving as a pap smear. Most people often equate these things (value systems, guidance, standards, and morality) as being controlling, which is why for some, rules are offensive, when the purpose of rules is to supply structure and organization. A girl/woman possessing a clear sense of direction, standards, or morals will continue to be an anomaly while secretly being revered.

But you must understand that the bad girl will be publically applauded for her boldness in wearing nothing under a sheer overlay, sleeping with a married man while shouting it loudly from her Facebook page, and single-handedly inspiring a culture of men to write songs supporting her pole swinging. However, secretly, their value will always be questioned. The "bad girl" will fight for the same respect of that of a "good girl."

The good girl won't get the song written about her, but she will get the middle finger quite often, as well as the occasional "female dog" reference. Let us not forget those who will make sure that the "good girl" questions herself by spewing at her, "Who told you that you were worth all that?!" or "You are not better than me!" There is really a battle being waged against morality, not really the "good girl" herself. But she will have to fight it just the same. Because she carries the mantle.

BRINGING IT ALL TOGETHER

What I found when I looked up the definition of conscience and decided to study it out was very interesting. The following definition comes from www.dictionary.com:

Conscience is defined as the inner sense of what is right or wrong in one's conduct (which is behavior), or motives (which is one's intentions) pushing one toward RIGHT actions.

How do you know what is the right action? Well, you will know because you won't have to question it. There is a flow accompanied by appropriate behavior when we are doing the right thing. And if you need further assistance with the simplicity of this premise, trust me that you will know when you are doing the right thing without a doubt because usually it does not initially or ONLY benefit YOU. I know this is a major paradigm shift because we are taught to consider only ourselves regarding justice.

God ALWAYS desires to have us do the right thing while balancing the scales so that the other parties or party involved is also BEING DONE RIGHT. God wants YOU to be treated right, as well as the next person. It is not only about you! Justice gets served when we move like this. If we were to be obedient TO INTEGRITY, revenge would be less necessary or warranted.

Also, doing the right thing puts us at rest. I'll say it again, the right actions puts US, (YOU) at rest. Rest has several definitions but the one that I am going to focus on is this one: relief or freedom, especially from anything that worries, troubles or disturbs. Let that sink in. When we listen to our conscience, we can have relief or freedom from anything that could worry, trouble, or disturb us.

The wrong actions vex us while consuming us with guilt, which results in an unrest, unrest meaning a lack of rest, a restless, troubled, or uneasy state. No matter whom you ask, regardless of culture, their consciences bear witness against or for their decisions. Their consciences either enter a state of rest or unrest.

Why don't writers or authors convey the brawl that occurs internally when a character chooses to sleep with a married man, or when a character chooses to have sex outside of marriage? Because the depth of an internal struggle (which is conscience based) indicates that there is a right or wrong to choose from that goes deeper than the desire to be pleased. So, the writer/author writes in a justification for the decision which yields the behavior and usually without eternal moral consequence being depicted.

If the writer/author do happen to convey a struggle, it then becomes very confused with freedom having the freedom to do it, turning away the attention from it being wrong.

Do not be fooled! Feelings do not make an action right. If they did, no one would be marching for the rights of the numerous black men being unjustly killed.

I have read articles where some of the accused police officers stated they FELT scared of the black suspect or intimidated which they had in custody. One would think that a TRAINED POLICE OFFICER would be able to handle a ***fearful feeling better.***

Know that God feels when we feel, but He has created a God-conscience on the inside of us to help guide us when it is about right or wrong and NOT feelings alone.

So, should feelings really be a viable excuse for a police officer to make a decision of life and death without at least trying to assess other variables of the situation? Where is the deductive reasoning? So, what's the excuse again, police officers, congress, senate, and so on?

I broke down the definition of conscience earlier in the text so you could see how it plainly speaks to the sense of right and wrong that everyone encounters regardless of their motives or conduct. No one is going to be able to make the "feelings excuse" with God. Our man-made laws unfortunately only allow room for that flaw. God knows us completely. Which means God knows us better than that. When we give permission for feelings alone to guide us, we give permission for the lack of full responsibility to be accepted.

Understand, the enemy can't afford to willingly let an awakening take place in our consciences. The television industry literally could not survive on a God-conscious awakened society. It would make them change what and how they write, and that would change what we crave, and that would change what makes money.

OOOOOH, now that's pressure that would, surely, burst a pipe!

NOTES

Date:_____Time:_____Mood:_____

_____
_____
_____
_____
_____
_____
_____
_____
_____
_____
_____
_____
_____
_____
_____
_____
_____
_____
_____

Chapter Four

RIGHTLY DIVIDING A FAD: HOW DO I DO THAT?

*E*verything is open for interpretation. I do mean everything! But know that not everything *tends to be interpreted correctly.*

Therefore, interpretation should be dissected with an honorable mind which can exercise objectivity so that the conclusion of the issues at hand will not be handled self-servingly or one-dimensionally, but just and fair. In this way, the interpretation can serve as a foundation upon which it will be able to withstand the poking and scoping of mere opinions and speculations. After all, opinions are subjective. Speculations can have us question the wrong thing. Facts are truth.

Let us get right into it. How does one rightly divide a fad? Let's begin with exploring the definition of FAD. There are two meanings which will be discussed, from two separate sources. It is not surprising that the two definitions share commonality because, of course, we are looking up the same word. However, the definitions do surprisingly and refreshingly highlight some foundational and certainly key components we need for a full understanding that the other source does not include.

FAD (Bing's Definition)

1) an intense and widely shared enthusiasm for something, especially one that is short-lived and without basis in the object's qualities; a craze

FAD (Wikipedia's Definition)

2) a fad or trend or craze is any form of collective behavior that develops within a culture, a generation or social group in which impulse is followed enthusiastically by a group of people for a finite period of time.

THE FACTS OF A FAD OUTLINED

A fad requires many (and many, by definition, does not note a concrete number) people to agree on it; "it" can be anything, "it" should have your excitement, "it" should have your commitment, "it" does not require reasoning to participate, and "it" will NOT last for a long period of time. And let's not forget, although not previously mentioned, a fad can return and die out multiple times, reinventing itself with slight changes.

Now let us go a little deeper to fully understand fad's definition by detailing the meaning of some of the words which make up and lie within the two definitions of FAD:

BASIS

1. anything upon which something is based;
groundwork; foundation

Have you ever stopped and inquired about the foundation of a fad? Where did it come from? How did it become

47

a fad? Does it have a purpose? I must be the first to raise my hand high while shaking my head NO! I honestly did not think it was important enough. Moving on.

CRAZE

1) to derange or impair the mind; make insane; impair to make or cause to become worse; diminish in ability, value, excellence, etc. (dictionary.com)

2) wildly insane or excited Someone reading this may be thinking, "But a fad impairs the mind in a good way." Advertisers would agree as they look at all those zeros on the check they receive for making sure their products and jingles get into our heads, thus ensuring it's created a feeling within us. Our minds and emotions are certainly their priority because they know actions will follow what we feel, and passionate feelings fuel our convictions.

So creating a CRAZE is the goal because a CRAZE stays in your mind, never leaves, and becomes a part of your memory and experience. Thus when the FAD resurfaces, your mind has a point of reference and familiarity. After all, people BUY and SUPPORT what they KNOW!

INSANITY

1. extreme foolishness; folly; senselessness

Right now, you are probably thinking, "Fads are not meant to make sense, and are intended to be fun!" I can earnestly tell you that I can understand why you might be thinking that. I can't, however, completely agree with the sentiment that FADS are about fun ONLY and are without intent or purpose. Simply put, everything has a purpose.

Extreme foolishness and folly do not require the use of common sense, common sense meaning sound judgment. The actions of someone acting foolishly do NOT compel them to think through their actions. Foolishness has been referred to as mindless behavior, behavior without a structured or moral compass or without care to conseJ quences.

In our society, can we really afford to be without our right mind, if even for a moment?

IMPULSE

1. the influence of a particular feeling or mental

state

We all deal with impulses every day. To be more accurate, I will say every minute. Think about the many things you feel like doing, and therefore most likely do, without ever considering the "why," especially when the boundary to NOT do it is NOT present.

INTENSE

1) strong sensations, feelings or emotions We are a few words into exploring the words that define the word FAD, and as you can see, we are still talking about feelings. It seems like you can't get away from it when it comes to fads. This powerfully lends insight into the emotional strength of a fad itself.

Did you think where it concerns your participation in a fad, that all of this was happening? Quite eye-opening, isn't it? I always hear people say, "It doesn't mean all of that," meaning to not take the subject at hand so seriously. On the contrary; know everything means something and that meaning deserves serious observation. So, don't be so quick to write off the value of thoroughly comprehending a thing, specifically when you are representing it.

It is vital you know how you are investing your energies and what they are requiring of you. You need to take note if it speaks to the quality of person you are or if it aligns with your values.

BRINGING IT ALL TOGETHER

We're not done quite yet. Let us take one more look into FAD. After defining the word FAD and the words which make it up, I then had to look up the synonyms of the word "fad." Synonyms are words that mean the same as the original word. Afterward, I explored the antonyms of the word FAD as well. Antonym means the opposite of a word. Let us proceed.

Synonyms of FAD (same as):
CRAZE, VOGUE, TREND, PASSION
Antonyms (opposites) of FAD:
STANDARD, TRADITION, HATE, BOREDOM

Strikingly enough, the words which mean the opposite of FAD are known in our society to NOT be good. It brings home the point I made referencing what I described as the good girl assassination. Because standard, tradition, hate, and boredom all now mean the same, or at the very *least have the same descriptive relationship to one another. When did that happen?*

Is every fad bad? No. Is it wrong to desire to be "in the know" of what is in style socially and or culturally? No. Having said that, there is still very much a need for us to be awake regarding what in a fad may cause us to negotiate our morals, compromise our values, or wholly ignore good judgment.

On the grounds of the previous statement, there is a need to ask, "Do you think you would be able to rightly divide a fad? Do you even want to rightly divide it?"

For some, life is better in the realm of the unknown. Those who choose the unknown do not realize it leaves them vulnerable to its impact.

Rightly dividing means to cut up or dissect. We must do this when fads are served to us.

I will say it again: there is a need for you and me to make good judgment calls with respect to what is in a fad, as it may cause us to negotiate our morals, compromise our values, or completely ignore good judgment.

TAKE ONLY WHAT YOU NEED

One Sunday, the First Lady of a church I belonged to came into the sanctuary with a symmetrical bob that complimented her amazingly well. It was gorgeous. She was already beautiful, and the hairstyle magnified it!

The following Sunday, at least fifty women came to church with a version of the same hairstyle! The reason why I say "version" is because it did not look the same on the others as it did on her. It varied a bit. To start with, the thickness of their hair was different, the starting length was different, their faces were different, all of which in the end impacted the overall look.

To make this a little more ironic. Some of the same women that copied the hairstyle even went so far as to purchase a similar outfit to what she had on that Sunday! I was like, whoa! My issue was that it was so obvious that they wanted her look, completely. Was it bad to emulate? Not necessarily. It was a hairstyle. But here is my point: where was their individuality? Where was their identity?

But let me tell you something ... something I hope we would get from seeing someone transform into the best version of themselves is the inspiration to establish our identity, and then leave out the pull to duplicate them. It is absolutely wonderful to be motivated to the freedom of attempting something different, while in the same breath not submit to the pressure to change who we are. Unfortunately, that is exactly what happens. It gets extreme! TAKE ONLY WHAT YOU NEED.

Is it possible to take the motivation of inspiration and propel it into something greater?! Only if the greater is seen and believed to be active and thriving by the individual being motivated and inspired for themselves. We do NOT want to undermine YOUR own ability to invoke significance in this world. Because you possess it too!

The next few questions are worth answering.

1) What fad are you supporting of your generation? 2) Why are you supporting it? 3) What is it costing you? 4) Have you lost yourself in it?

Remember, fads will come and go. Fads are intended to influence. But rightly divide it! No fad should make you compromise your God-given conscience, good girl. If it tries to, it is not for you.

NOTES

Date:_____Time:_____Mood:_____

_____

_____

_____

_____

_____

_____

_____

_____

_____

_____

_____

_____

_____

_____

_____

Chapter Five

STAND FIRM IN YOUR PUMPS

J don't want you to make the mistake of thinking that standing on morality and ethics is going to be easy. You must be committed to it. In addition, you must also be committed to the *"why"* of your convictions. Also, your convictions should be firm, able to withstand diverse opinions which will challenge its validity and importance. You must understand this. This declaration is for YOU: *I will be committed to the "why" of my convictions!*

James 1:6-8 speaks about allowing a man to ask for anything with their faith solely in God while not doubting. It goes on to say that a man who doubts is like a wave of the sea, driven and tossed by the wind. The term "man" used in this scripture equally qualifies a "woman." So yes, good girl, this applies to you.

This scripture can also read like this: If you, woman, doubt what you are having faith for, you are likened to a wave of the sea, driven and tossed by the wind. If you read a little further down from that passage, which would be James 1:9, it goes on to state a person that is tossed by the sea is double-minded and unstable in all their ways. For this reason, YOU must make up YOUR mind.

After maturing and having to examine myself regarding my own double-mindedness, I understand the relevance of this passage like never before. Our double-mindedness as believers frequently comes from the lack of trust we have in God, which is the crux of our salvation and faith. We are saved once we believe in our hearts and confess with our mouths that Jesus Christ hung on the cross, died, and rose again on the third day with all power in His hands.

To believe in a thing means to trust in a thing. Trusting a thing means being able to rely and stand _on its strength._ God's strength is a fable to some people because they cannot seem to see it with their naked eyes, and if you can't see something whether physically or in your heart, you definitely won't be able to recognize it.

Allow me please to show you where you are missing it at...

The visibility of God's strength can be contributed to many things, like the fact that God's strength sustains, maintains, comforts, pushes, holds back, loves hard, forgives quickly, and takes responsibility for what most people hide from. Strength cannot always be identified in a muscular physique, or muscular strength itself. Although these attributes of physical strength and build are great, they are not equipped to withstand what the heart deals with in life. This is a spiritual thing. It is not a physical one.

When we trust God for real, we are rooted and cannot be uprooted unless we move. Wind can be felt, but not seen unless its presence is seen in the movement of rolling hay down a street, the sway of trees, the ripple of a stream, or the diagonal fall of the rain.

Have you ever met someone that changes their minds more than they are sure of themselves? They will re-ask something again and again. They will question their own certainty. Then, they will change their minds from their original decision only to come back it later. It showcases the uncertainty which is at the foundation of every one of their decisions.

You can be assured since this is the case, there is a string of instability that can be seen throughout their lives as a whole. I call them "Wind People." Wind People are those who are tossed back and forth not sometimes, but all the time and in no certain area of their lives. Additionally, they tend to operate in indecisiveness in various areas of their lives which yields a lack of progression. Wind People are always finding themselves stuck somewhere.

HOLD TIGHT TO THESE TIPS

- Do not sway. Stand firm in your decisions. Know why you are committing to an attitude or behavior.
- Be aware of what your convictions or beliefs stand upon. Do not forget to review them every three to six months. It will not only keep you on track, but focus you.
- Be mindful that you will evolve and grow during your life, but convictions and beliefs should aid you in stabilizing that journey of growth, NOT toss you back and forth or engage you in non-fruitful negotiations.
- There will be so many things that will tell you to bend. Be flexible, not breakable.
- Be careful of being fooled by slick speech. It can sound good, but do not forget to rightly divide

what you are listening to. Break it down. Ask questions. There is nothing wrong with that. One thing is for sure: a lie cannot withstand too much questioning, dissecting, or repetition. Remember, a lie will break down without much effort, especially when the truth of a matter is sought out.

- Be sure not to be so quick to succumb to what "sounds good." Listen closer so you can hear caution when it speaks.

VIBING WITH YOU

There were instances where my daughter, then just a teenager, wanted to go out with her friends and I did not allow her to go. When her friends came back to gloat about how much fun they had, she would say, "See, Mom! Nothing bad happened! I could have gone!"

From a parent's point of view, the "going" wasn't or isn't always the issue. Unbeknownst to her, I was not only careful about what she experienced, but who she experienced it with. That can make all the difference!

Attending a wild college party with a good friend with their head on straight can be survived, but attending that same wild party with a party animal can have you wrangling in a drunken friend or worse, in an accident where a loss of life could occur.

Understand that wisdom comes from God. And wisdom operates to give us insight to a divine perspective. The word says ask for wisdom and God will generously supply it to you.

Be wise about who you're vibing with. Keep in mind that connections are made a million times a day through Facebook, Twitter, and Instagram. Think about some of the things that get posted. If you had to be judged by your associations through these mediums, would you be okay with that?

Most of us who loosely guard our interactions would say yes. Why? Because these people are not familiar to you, and therefore you do not feel responsible for what they share. With that being said, should you? Read the example below and see if you still feel the same way.

My friend, Pat, would do this one really awesome demonstration as part of her lesson to the ladies. It is going to really bring my point home regarding the possible contamination of connections.

Pat would lay out all the ingredients for making some pretty yummy chocolate chip cookies before us, her audience. She added the chocolate chips, flour, sugar, and other needed items. Pat made it soooo enticing!

We definitely wanted a cookie until ... She reached behind her to grab a bag. It was a clear bag. Everyone wondered what it was for as we started to look around at one another to see if anyone could recognize its content.

Then Pat said, "Oh, let me reach in and get some of my dog's poop out of this bag."

She was so calm. We were all gagging! She quickly

opened the bag and put the poop right into the bowl with everything else!

Pat went on to say, "You notice how the poop was not on the table with the other ingredients; it was hidden. For that matter, it was individually wrapped and the smell was masked so it would not announce its presence."

Everyone in the room was like, "Noooo! Ewww! Gross!" Pat looked us all in the eye while asking, "So, do you still want some cookies?"

We screamed, "Noooo!" She did not react to our dismay. She calmly continued to make the cookies, poop and all.

Pat said, "Well, that is what we do. We tolerate a little poop in with the good stuff in our lives all the time."

She kept combining the ingredients as the crowd continued to react all the more. Then she said, "When it is mixed in, you won't know it's there."

Pat could not pay anyone to eat those cookies! Nevertheless, the point was made.

We tolerate the poop. We would like to think that if we had foreknowledge of the poop, it would make a difference. The truth is, in most cases, it doesn't. Just like the preacher's son that knows every scripture but also knows every word of "Four Play" by R. Kelly, or the best friend that gets straights A's but knows how to turn it up like nobody's business, or the friend that is super rich but likes to shoplift for the thrill. Shoplifting, heavily charged sexual content, and being an out of control partier are the non-visible character poop that we often tolerate. And guess what ... we eat the cookies anyway! We hang out with that friend anyway. We continue to buy the music with no ethical or moral value anyway.

There are indeed instances where we don't know the poop is in the cookies, but we have a sense something isn't right, but won't probe because we're scared of what we will find out! Like the "wonderful man" you will meet, good girl. He will be available by phone. He will take you out to lunch three out of the seven days a week. He will initially be very attentive. However, you'll begin to notice that he never seems to call after 10PM.

Or maybe, you are up late tonight, good girl, and you want to talk. His phone is going directly to voicemail. You ignore it at first, but then it turns into a trend.

Good girl, let's also look at the man that is around a little too much. You have been going out with him for nine months. When month five rolled around, he suddenly fell on hard times and moved in with you. He says he's looking for a job. He has not found one yet. Bills are due, and YOU are the only one paying them.

Lastly, let's look at the man that has been engaged four times before he met you. You begin to notice a pattern in which his engagements only last three to four months at a time. You refuse to ask needed questions because you don't want to mess it up. He has proposed to you and you have accepted. But he has you convinced that he has been the victim in those previous engagements. Again I ask, "Why won't you inquire further?"

I cannot say it enough! Rightly divide what you are

being told and ask the necessary follow-up questions! Are you single? Are you emotionally single? Do you have a wife? Are you divorced? Where do you live? What financial obligations do you currently have? How long have you been on your job? What is the last church service you attended? What was the message about? How do you feel about honesty? What is your perspective on adultery?

Good girl, I want to caution YOU as well not to play games with anyone's mind. Be honest. Be direct. Know where you stand. Be willing to be reasonably open. Be willing to answer the same questions. Don't waiver.

Knowing who you are as a woman is one of the most amazing and powerful things you can be. It automatically eliminates you in most cases from being chosen by the men that need to sup from you. Knowing who you are will keep you from being abused by a young man that says you make him so mad it forces him to strike you.

Stand firm in your pumps. Know your identity. Know your boundaries. Review your boundaries. Avoid being flakey. If you show that you are not sure, that can give people the impression that they need to make your mind up for you. And let's be honest, you don't need that. You are capable of thinking for yourself.

NOTES

Date:_____Time:_____Mood:_____

_____
_____
_____
_____
_____
_____
_____
_____
_____
_____
_____
_____
_____
_____
_____
_____

Chapter Six

GOOD GIRL VS. BAD GIRL

he heat of this comparison has been brewing and brewing, yet no one has talked about it: Good Girl VS Bad Girl.

It has been a long time coming. The "bad girl" has been all up in your face, accusing you of thinking that you are better than her. She, the "bad girl," wants you to know your man prefers her twerk to your hallelujah. Not to mention that she also desires to remind you that just because you are good, doesn't mean your man will love you more or be faithful to you.

On the other hand, the "good girl," without pointing her fingers or rolling her neck, wants the "bad girl" to know that when this man is through with you, he will come back to her. Lest you forget that he won't bring you home to meet his mama. The "good girl" will tell you that she is classy and feels you act less than that.

Yet and still, the "good girl" is secretly ticked and perhaps a bit threatened because of what her beliefs restrict her in doing, what she feels guilty about doing, or plain ol' afraid to do.

She knows that history has proven the "bad girl" will do "it" without guilt or shame. Yes, the "bad girl" will do what you won't. She will twist, twerk, and jerk. This "bad girl" will wear a provocative outfit with no apologies or regrets.

She seems to be free. The "good girl" seems to be shackled. Who is what, really?

The truth is that the good girl versus bad girl has been an unspoken rivalry for a long time. It is not just about the Good Girl versus Bad Girl title, but at the root of it all, it is about morals and immorality, who has it and who doesn't. Please read on.

I had a discussion with a single woman recently. I need to mention for reasons that will become obvious that she is over fifty years of age. As single women do, she is dating but feels that even at her age, she is coming up against some real feelings of competition with other women. Not just any women, but the women she calls "bad girls" that she doesn't even know.

Let's call her Vera. What's Vera's gripe? Here we go... The guy Vera is dating is handsome, kind, wealthy, a Christian, and over fifty himself. On the surface, they really are a good match. Vera knows he has his pick of the litter. At the same time, she does not hesitate to express that she is the crème of the crop of the litter he's choosing from.

However, Vera wants it known she is a woman of standards. She is an ordained Pastor, very attractive, degreed, and full of life. Nevertheless, the feelings of empowerment fade when she thinks of the pool of men she has to choose from, because the qualifications she has will eliminate many by default. In fact, they already have.

Vera knows from her prior dealings with this man that their relationship will only work if he commits. She also recalls how good he is in bed when they had their prior dealings. Vera, this "good girl/woman," wants to do it honorably this time. No sex before commitment. She told me explicitly, "I am too old for that!"

Vera made it abundantly clear that the decision of abstinence definitely threatened the potential of the outcome she desired, which is a relationship leading to marriage with this guy because of his options to not have to wait on a woman. But she feels even more of a threat to her are the "bad girls" who she knows are willing to forfeit their standards of commitment and honor to please him sexually.

Vera knows she is in a tug-of-war between her morals, loneliness, and her desires. Vera said bluntly that what is between her legs has not made the same commitment. So, it gets tough. Insecurity has begun to set in. She wants to try and keep his attention without coming across as clingy, because in her words, "My vagina won't be on his mind due to the fact he isn't getting it, so my voice needs to stay in his ear."

But again, she doesn't want to be a nag. The "bad girl"

made her nervous. She kept bringing "her" up. The nameless and faceless "bad girl" was her nemesis and she didn't even know her. But still, she hated her and the fact she had to go up against her.

I learned so much from this conversation. The 3D picture that was painted by this conversation made it very tangible that rivalry between women was more than about looks. It included character. Think about it; the Side Chick VS The Wife; The Girlfriend VS The Friend With Benefits; and especially, The Baby Mama VS The New Woman.

Immorality is always going to get the shock value because it is often painted as the fun path, but it does not tell the whole truth. The side you don't see is the impact of their screaming consciences which result in the restless nights, confused minds, tears and lots of joyless times. Immorality will snuff out your integrity and have you compromising what stabilizes you and your identity. Immorality can't tell you everything it has up its sleeve. If it did, it would not be as alluring. Full disclosure isn't a part of the deal.

Good girl, your opposition is not the "bad girl" or the woman with no morality or standards. The fight is within you because you have made her your competition unfairly. Quality will always outlast cheap. Morality will continually be what a man desires most to take home to his family.

So, remove yourself as the bad girl's opponent and embrace her. Your rivalry will continue to drive a wedge between the solidarity women should be embracing. We should have each other's back enough to tell a flirting married man to go home to his wife or make it clear that you will be no one's side-piece. We as women should respect the next woman, no matter the race, not because we know her, but because you love yourself enough not to destroy some else's home, remove someone's father from the home, or be used to plant a seed of abandonment in another woman's heart.

THE TRUTH IS your prayers are needed. Your ethics are needed. Your unwavering agreeability regarding who you are is needed.

Good girl, remember you are supposed to be the light of the world.

YOU ARE TO BE THE EXAMPLE, NOT SIT ON A PEDESTAL. DON'T FIGHT HER, EMBRACE HER.

NOTES

Date:_____Time:_____Mood:_____

_____

_____

_____

_____

_____

_____

_____

_____

_____

_____

_____

_____

_____

_____

_____

_____

THANK EACH OF YOU ABUNDANTLY

God I do not have words to fully describe the love I have grown to have for You. You have matured me, kept love, loved me, encouraged me, rebuked me, corrected me, told me to apologize, caused me to reflect on my character, stabilized me and my mind, strengthened me, sharpened me, gutted me clean and reassembled me for greatness. You are the reason I can write. Writing was the gift you generously gave to me and I thank YOU from everything that is within me! ***It is Your anointing flowing through my pen!*** I know You are real God. Jesus, You were not just a man. Holy Spirit I need you everyday!

To my husband Pastor Allen K Hunter, you have really exceeded my wildest dreams regarding how much you believe in me, my talents, gifts, and in my mantle as a scribe. I can tell you that you push me beyond what I want at times, but you must know it exactly what I need most of the time.

You have made sure that my dream came before yours. You sowed and sowed so I could get to the next level. You have un-selfishlessly sowed your gifts into my life. You have blessed my life! And I love you, I really do!

To my mommy I love you so much! You have given me so much of what I attribute my ability to be the caliber of woman today that you are so proud of. You have held me when I cried and corrected me when I was out of line. And still to this day is willing to fight for me. Your strength amazes me and your ability to push through your own circumstances to live your best life. I am proud of you and thank you for paving the way educationally for me and breaking the educational curse! Congratulations on a job well done as a Mom! You are loved by me!

To my daughter Zee you are the reason that I could not see myself being anything else but a good mother. I saw in you all the greatness anyone could ever see in their child, and because of that I knew you would do great things! I knew you would grow to be beautiful and intelligent and such a go-getter! I thank you for loving me and encouraging me in the writing of this book. Your contribution helped make it better. Your presence in my life is irreplaceable I love you my Panda!

To my cousin Theo I appreciate you so much! You have sown into me above and beyond the call of duty. You have given when I did not have anything. You supported me, listened to me, loved me, pushed me and was just there when I needed you. I will never forget the impact you have made in my life and the care you have shown me and my entire family. You are loved by me!

To Paulette, since we meet you have inspired me to go beyond myself. You have consistently spoken God's word and love into my life. Know, your friendship is so very important to me. It have superseded distance and it has weathered the storms we have experienced in each of our lives. Thank you so much for sharing your gift, talent and love. You are amazing and I love you!

ABOUT THE AUTHOR
Author Jay Doubleu

Author Jay Doubleu is described as one of the most authentic and sincere writers of her time. She is known by readers as a passionate believer of God and His Word. She skillfully pens that passion in the most welcoming of way, which allows anyone to be able to pick up her book and connect with her.

Her freshman novel entitled "HOPE Exposed" was inspired by her journey to understand her present circumstances, and a traumatic divorce while remaining a fighter through it all. Author Jay is purposeful in her tone, her intent and her mandate as an author. Her sophomore release is entitled "Okay to Be a Good Girl" already being noticed for its attention grabbing title.

She is planning to also release two more books within the next year. Both will be sure to stir the soul, ignite the fire of motivation and comfort the hearts of the readers. She has got so much to give to the world, and she has no plans to stop anytime soon. Author Jay Double also holds three degrees including Bachelors in Communications/Journalism, a Graduate degree in Urban Planning and currently pursuing a Masters in Couples and Family Therapy.

Made in the USA
Middletown, DE
11 June 2019